# DOGS SET VI

# LHASA APSOS

Nancy Furstinger
ABDO Publishing Company

# visit us at
# www.abdopub.com

Published by ABDO Publishing Company, 4940 Viking Drive, Edina, Minnesota 55435.
Copyright © 2006 by Abdo Consulting Group, Inc. International copyrights reserved in
all countries. No part of this book may be reproduced in any form without written
permission from the publisher. The Checkerboard Library™ is a trademark and logo of
ABDO Publishing Company.

Printed in the United States.

Cover Photo: Corbis
Interior Photos: Corbis pp. 5, 9, 11, 17, 20; Getty Images pp. 7, 14; PhotoEdit pp. 13, 19,
    21; SuperStock pp. 12, 15

Series Coordinator: Megan M. Gunderson
Editors: Heidi M. Dahmes, Megan M. Gunderson
Art Direction: Neil Klinepier

## Library of Congress Cataloging-in-Publication Data

Furstinger, Nancy.
    Lhasa apsos / Nancy Furstinger.
        p. cm. -- (Dogs. Set VI)
    Includes index.
    ISBN 1-59679-271-X
    1. Lhasa apso--Juvenile literature. I. Title.

    SF429.L5F87 2005
    636.72--dc22

                                                                2005042130

# CONTENTS

# THE DOG FAMILY

Dogs have lived with humans for at least 12,000 years. They were among the first tamed animals. Ancient people, such as the Egyptians, saw these **domesticated** dogs as sacred. Today, they are our best friends, hunting partners, and protectors.

Almost 400 different **breeds** of dogs exist worldwide. Dogs come in many colors, shapes, and sizes. Each has been bred for special reasons, such as pulling sleds and herding sheep.

Despite their different appearances, all dogs belong to the Canidae **family**. This name comes from the Latin word *canis*, which means "dog." The Canidae family also includes coyotes, foxes, jackals, and wolves.

Dogs and wolves still share common features. They both communicate through howling and growling. And, they both have advanced smelling and hearing capabilities.

# LHASA APSOS

Lhasa Apsos were first **bred** in Tibet in the 700s BC. Monks raised these dogs to be interior guards in Lhasa, Tibet's capital.

In this wild mountain country, they were known as *abso seng kye*. This means "bark lion sentinel dog." Watchfulness and keen hearing made Lhasa Apsos well suited for watchdog duty.

Lhasa Apsos were never sold, and only left Tibet as gifts of good fortune. The first pair in the United States was sent to Suydam Cutting of New Jersey in 1933. They were a gift from his acquaintance the thirteenth Dalai Lama, Tibet's spiritual leader.

In 1935, the breed was recognized by the **American Kennel Club (AKC)**. This means **purebred** Lhasa Apsos can compete in AKC events.

Tibet is known as "the roof of the world." Lhasa Apsos are still raised there.

# What They're Like

This small dog has a big dog attitude. According to legend, when a Lhasa Apso looks in a mirror, he sees a lion. This is one reason the **breed** earned the nickname "little lion dog."

Lhasa Apsos can be lively and headstrong. However, training and patience can prevent bad behavior. These dogs are intelligent and are quick learners.

Lhasa Apsos also have the heart of a clown. One of their tricks is climbing up to a high perch. These little lion dogs have no fear of heights.

Lhasa Apso eyes are often hidden under a mane of fur!

# COAT AND COLOR

The Lhasa Apso has a thick coat that flows straight to the ground. Facial fur forms a beard and whiskers. This heavy coat protected these dogs from Tibet's cold winters.

Heavy hair hangs over a Lhasa Apso's ears and eyes. This **fall** of fur shields its dark brown eyes from wind and sunlight. But, it is still able to see because long eyelashes keep this hair out of its eyes.

The fur is parted from the top of the Lhasa Apso's black nose to the base of its tail. Long hair flows from the tail, which forms a screwlike curl over the back.

A Lhasa Apso's coat can be any color. But, the lionlike golden color is the most popular shade. Some dogs have dark tips decorating their ears and beards.

A Lhasa Apso's fur is often trimmed evenly to floor-length. This way, it doesn't get dirty as quickly.

# SIZE

The Lhasa Apso is a small **breed**.  But, they are big enough to carry out their watchdog duties!  In addition to being compact, Lhasa Apsos have muscled bodies.

Lhasa Apsos are known for protecting people.  They may bark at strangers until they know everyone is safe, especially at home.

**Letting your Lhasa Apso run and play will help it maintain a healthy weight.**

Males stand about 10 or 11 inches (25 or 28 cm) tall at the shoulders. Females stand slightly shorter. On average, Lhasa Apsos weigh between 13 and 19 pounds (6 and 9 kg).

# CARE

Lhasa Apsos need to be groomed regularly to keep their fur shiny and tangle free.  Use a special dog brush and comb to remove knots from the fur.

**Grooming is a major part of dog show competitions.**

When bathing, squeeze shampoo through the coat in a downward motion. After rinsing, blow-dry completely while brushing the fur in layers.

Use the end tooth of a comb to part the hair down your Lhasa Apso's back.  Finish with a topknot, using ribbons or barrettes to keep the hair

out of its eyes. Dogs not competing in an **AKC** dog show can visit the groomer for a short trim.

Like all dogs, a Lhasa Apso needs to visit the veterinarian at least once each year. They will make certain your pet is healthy and up-to-date on **vaccines**. The veterinarian can also **spay** or **neuter** your pet.

A shorter puppy clip and regular baths help keep a Lhasa Apso clean.

# FEEDING

When you bring your Lhasa Apso home, feed it the same food it has been eating. Continue with this diet, or slowly mix in a new food. A gradual change can prevent stomach upsets.

Feed your new pet a dog food that provides balanced nutrition. The label will guide you on how much and how often to feed your dog. These guidelines are based on its age and weight.

Lhasa Apsos like to follow a set pattern. Serve the food at the same time every day. And, always have clean, fresh water available.

In between meals, your dog will enjoy healthy snacks. Dog biscuits can help keep teeth clean. Most dogs love bones, too. But, bones can splinter and harm your dog. Nylon bones or rawhide chews are safer.

*Dog food comes in dry, semimoist, and canned forms. A veterinarian can suggest the proper food for each pet.*

# THINGS THEY NEED

Lhasa Apsos adore attention. They have playful spirits and quickly learn tricks. They need positive and firm training. These dogs are very obedient to people they trust, such as their owners.

In order to stay healthy, Lhasa Apsos need regular exercise. A daily walk suits these sturdy dogs. Attach a nylon or leather leash to your dog's collar.

Your Lhasa Apso's collar should contain a license and a tag. The tag should include your dog's name, as well as your address and phone number. This will be helpful if your pet is lost.

After exercise, Lhasa Apsos need a peaceful place to sleep. Put a dog bed in a safe spot. Some dogs prefer to relax in a crate, which acts as a den. A dog toy will keep your pet company.

*Daily exercise helps keep a Lhasa Apso healthy.*

# PUPPIES

Baby dogs are called puppies. A mother dog carries her puppies inside her for about nine weeks. Like other small dogs, Lhasa Apsos have an average of one to four puppies in a **litter**.

Puppies spend their time sleeping, nursing, and growing. They open their eyes after about ten days. Puppies can walk at three weeks old. And, they are usually **weaned** at about six weeks of age.

When they are between 8 and 12 weeks old, puppies can go to their new homes. **Purebred** Lhasa Apsos can

*Lhasa Apso puppies are born in a wide range of colors.*

Rescue organizations are where dogs stay between homes. Lhasa Apso puppies and adults can be adopted from these places.

be bought from a qualified **breeder**. Lhasa Apsos can also be adopted from rescue organizations such as the **Humane Society**.

Take your puppy to a veterinarian, who will give it **vaccines** and check for worms. With proper care, a healthy Lhasa Apso will live about 12 to 14 years.

# GLOSSARY

**American Kennel Club (AKC)** - an organization that studies and promotes interest in purebred dogs.

**breed** - a group of animals sharing the same appearance and characteristics. A breeder is a person who raises animals. Raising animals is often called breeding them.

**domestic** - animals that are tame.

**fall** - something that hangs down, especially hair or fabric.

**family** - a group that scientists use to classify similar plants or animals. It ranks above a genus and below an order.

**Humane Society** - an organization that protects and cares for animals.

**litter** - all of the puppies born at one time to a mother dog.

**neuter** (NOO-tuhr) - to remove a male animal's
   reproductive organs.

**purebred** - an animal whose parents are both from the
   same breed.

**spay** - to remove a female animal's reproductive organs.

**vaccine** (vak-SEEN) - a shot given to animals or humans
   to prevent them from getting an illness or disease.

**wean** - to accustom an animal to eat food other than its
   mother's milk.

# WEB SITES

To learn more about Lhasa Apsos, visit ABDO Publishing
Company on the World Wide Web at **www.abdopub.com**.
Web sites about Lhasa Apsos are featured on our Book
Links page. These links are routinely monitored and
updated to provide the most current information
available.

# INDEX

**A**
adoption  20, 21
American Kennel
    Club  6, 15

**B**
bed  19

**C**
Canidae  4
character  8, 16, 18
coat  10, 14
collar  18
color  4, 10
coyote  4
Cutting, Suydam  6

**D**
Dalai Lama  6

**E**
ears  10
Egypt  4
exercise  18, 19
eyes  10, 15, 20

**F**
food  16
fox  4

**G**
grooming  14, 15
guarding  4, 6, 12

**H**
health  15, 16, 18,
    21
history  4, 6
hunting  4

**J**
jackal  4

**L**
leash  18
life span  21

**N**
neuter  15
nose  10

**P**
puppies  20, 21

**S**
size  4, 12, 13, 16
spay  15

**T**
tail  10
teeth  16
Tibet  6, 10
topknot  14
toys  19
training  8, 18
tricks  8, 18

**U**
United States  6

**V**
veterinarian  15, 21

**W**
water  16
wolf  4

24